Dehydrator Cookbook for Beginners

Dehydrator Cookbook for Beginners

365-Day Healthy, Delicious Recipes to Dehydrate Fruit, Vegetables, Meat & More | The Must-Have Bible for Beginners and Advanced Users

Atthew Fones

© Copyright 2021 Atthew Fones - All Rights Reserved.

In no way is it legal to reproduce, duplicate, or transmit any part of this document by either electronic means or in printed format. Recording of this publication is strictly prohibited, and any storage of this material is not allowed unless with written permission from the publisher. All rights reserved.

The information provided herein is stated to be truthful and consistent, in that any liability, regarding inattention or otherwise, by any usage or abuse of any policies, processes, or directions contained within is the solitary and complete responsibility of the recipient reader. Under no circumstances will any legal liability or blame be held against the publisher for any reparation, damages, or monetary loss due to the information herein, either directly or indirectly.

Respective authors own all copyrights not held by the publisher.

Legal Notice:

This book is copyright protected. This is only for personal use. You cannot amend, distribute, sell, use, quote or paraphrase any part of the content within this book without the consent of the author or copyright owner. Legal action will be pursued if this is breached.

Disclaimer Notice:

Please note the information contained within this document is for educational and entertainment purposes only. Every attempt has been made to provide accurate, up-to-date and reliable, complete information. No warranties of any kind are expressed or implied. Readers acknowledge that the author is not engaging in the rendering of legal, financial, medical or professional advice.

By reading this document, the reader agrees that under no circumstances are we responsible for any losses, direct or indirect, which are incurred as a result of the use of information contained within this document, including, but not limited to, errors, omissions, or inaccuracies.

TABLE OF CONTENTS

INTRODUCTION 008

CHAPTER 1: UNDERSTANDING THE FOOD DEHYDRATOR .009
- How Does It Work? 010
- Best Foods to Dehydrate 010
- FAQs About Using a Dehydrator 012

CHAPTER 2: MEAT 014
- Sweet & Sour Pork 015
- Smoked Herbed Bacon Jerky 016
- Venison Jerky 017
- Vietnamese Beef Jerky 018
- Paprika Pork Jerky 019
- Beer Beef Jerky 020
- Fish Teriyaki Jerky 021
- Pork Jerky in Chipotle Sauce 022
- Beef Teriyaki Jerky 023
- Beef Jerky 024
- Mustard Beef Jerky with Balsamic Vinegar 025
- Cajun Fish Jerky 026
- Lamb Jerky 027
- Beef Bulgogi Jerky 028
- Candied Bacon 029
- Buffalo Jerky 030
- Salmon Jerky 031
- Hickory Smoked Jerky 032
- Barbecue Beef Jerky 033
- Lemon Fish Jerky 034

CHAPTER 3: FRUITS 035
- Plum & Grape Fruit Leather 036
- Blackberry & Blueberry Fruit Rolls 037
- Raspberry Rolls 038
- Choco Bananas 039
- Berry Fruit Leather 040
- Dried Apple Chips with Cinnamon 041
- Candied Pumpkin 042
- Cinnamon Apple Chips 043
- Dried Mangoes 044

Fruit Leather 045
Blackberry Tuile 046
Dried Kiwi 047
Honey Peaches with Bourbon 048
Dried Papaya Cubes 049
Apple Fruit Leather 050
Peanut Butter & Banana Leather 051
Hazelnut Banana Leather 052
Dried Lemon 053
Dried Strawberries 054
Orange Fruit Leather 055

CHAPTER 4: VEGETABLES 056

Dried Sweet Potato 057
Broccoli & Cashew Bites 058
Paprika Zucchini 059
Crunchy Green Peas 060
Maple Carrot Straws 061
Cucumber Chips 062
Dehydrated Asparagus 063
Lemon Kale 064
Shawarma Kale 065
Spicy Garlic Kale 066
Spiced Cucumbers 067
Zucchini Snacks 068
Dehydrated Okra 069
Green Bean Crisps 070
Dehydrated Tomatoes 071
Dehydrated Pizza Broccoli 072
Dehydrated Corn 073
Dehydrated Beets 074
Dried Cauliflower Popcorn 075
Ranch Carrot 076

CHAPTER 5: HERBS & POWDER 077

Tomato Powder 078
Onion Powder 079
Powdered Ginger 080
Dried Parsley, Basil & Oregano Powder 081
Mushroom Powder 082
Dried Herb Mix 083

Thyme, Garlic, Rosemary & Lemon Herb Mix 084
Taco Seasoning 085
Onion & Garlic Powder Mix 086
Dried Herbs For Salad 087
Kimchi Powder 088
Herbes de Provence 089
Parsley, Oregano, Basil, Thyme & Red Pepper Herb Mix 090
Garlic Powder 091
Lemon Powder 092
Dried Basil Powder 093
Leek Powder 094
Italian Seasoning Blend 095
Basil, Marjoram & Sage Herb Mix 096
Porcini Cubes 097

CHAPTER 6: CRACKERS 098

Carrot Crackers 099
Sesame & Carrot Crackers 100
Green Crackers 101
Mexican Crackers 102
Peanut Butter & Banana Crackers 103
Flax Crackers 104
Seaweed & Tamari Crackers 105
Onion & Nut Crackers 106
Seed Crackers 107
Tomato & Flaxseed Crackers 108

CONCLUSION 109

INTRODUCTION

Dehydrating food has existed for thousands of years. The earliest forms of food dehydration were natural solar and air drying, where people exposed raw ingredients or brine-washed food to the sun and hot air for long periods. But in the modern day, there are so many different brilliant ways to dehydrate your food and make the most of your money!

Whether grow-your-own, bought locally from a farmer's market, or fresh from a regular supermarket, seasonality still affects the quality, abundance and price of good food. It just makes sense to preserve food quality for those times when it's not as plentiful or not available at all. Dehydrating food with this terrific book is easy and creates tasty food year-round.

This dehydrator cookbook includes easy instructions for cooking, dehydrating, storing, and reconstituting all kinds of foods. Choose the perfect dishes to keep your body fueled while you trek and learn how to pack provisions efficiently.

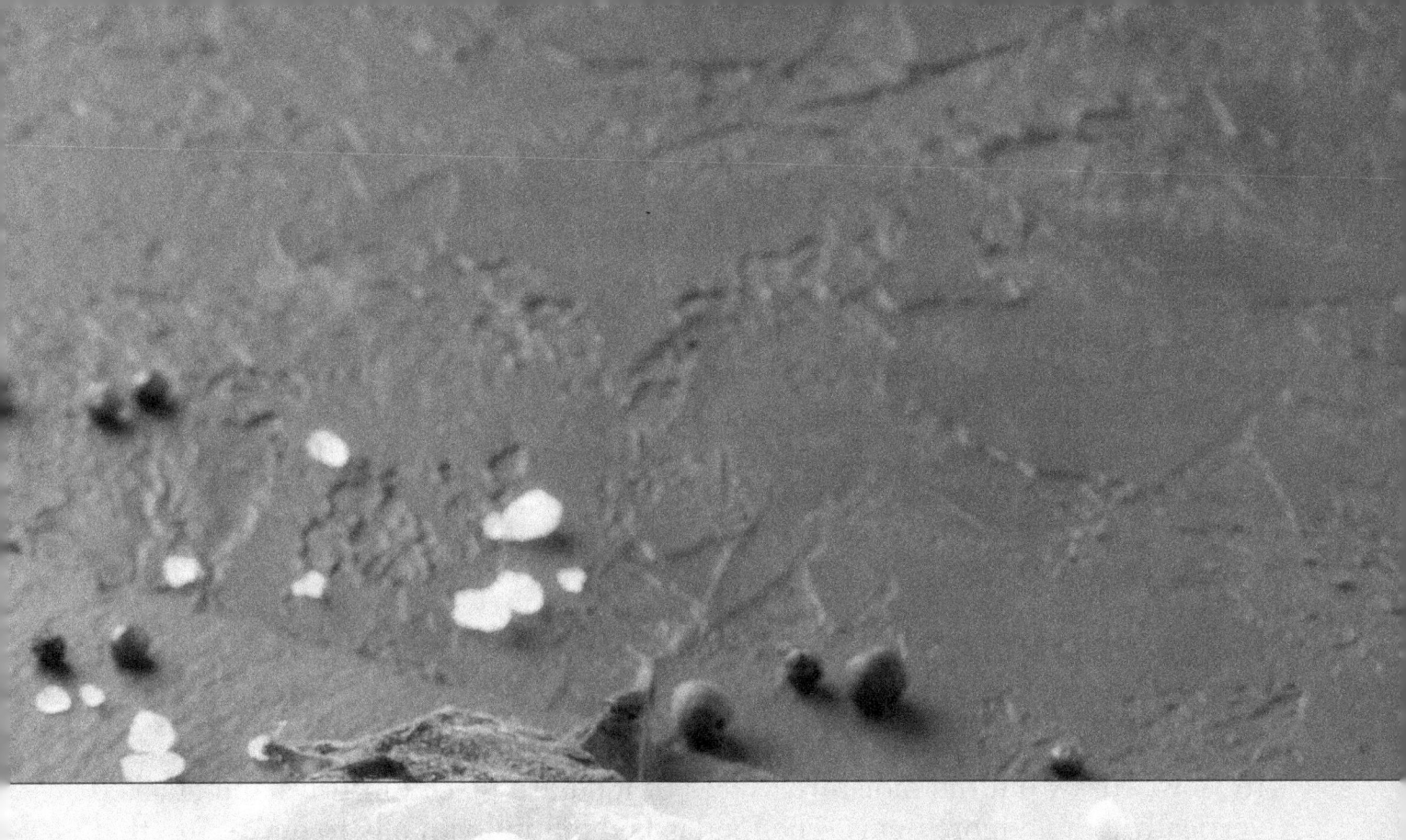

CHAPTER 1: UNDERSTANDING THE FOOD DEHYDRATOR

In food processing, dehydration refers to the method of completely or partially removing the moisture from the food in order to preserve it.

Moist or wet environments are prone to the growth of microorganisms like bacteria, mold, and yeast that cause spoilage.

There are various ways to draw out the moisture, and some methods are better than others in retaining the nutrients and flavors. While sun-drying and air-drying are common practices in most cultures, modern means of dehydration by using electricity proves to be convenient in most households. It not only saves space, but is quicker, more consistent, and reliable.

How Does It Work?

Electric food dehydrators are similar to convection ovens since they apply indirect heat to food through hot circulating air.

The main difference is that dehydrators use low heat and requires a longer time to slowly draw out the moisture. Slices of food are placed in trays and stacked vertically to hold more items. The food is laid out individually to make sure that they get even drying.

The heating elements in the dehydrator will heat up the air inside the chamber. Fans will then help the hot air get evenly distributed and slowly dry the food until all moisture is gone. Food items will reduce in size and become crispy as it loses its water content.

Time and temperature are two important factors in dehydration as it requires a slow process to maintain the flavors.

By removing the water content, you are left with flavors that are richer and enhanced. Getting moisture out and exposing food to hot air is also excellent at killing off harmful microorganisms. Food dehydrators also provides a customizable timer and thermostat to let you get the best results each time.

Best Foods to Dehydrate

Fruits

The best fruits to dehydrate are the ones that are in season. You'll be able to get more for a lower price and enjoy them for longer.

It's also a good way to save them from deteriorating. Dehydrate your remaining or overripe stocks to create sweet teas, fruit pies, candy alternatives, healthy chips, and more. Whenever you can, always opt for organic produce to get the maximum health benefits.

Bananas, pineapples, berries, grapes, oranges, peaches, and watermelons are among the best fruits to dehydrate. Just remember to not add any fresh fruit in your current drying batch as it will introduce moisture.

Vegetables

Dried vegetables can be added to your stocks, stews, broths, and soups, especially when they are not available in the market or are expensive. Like fruits, you may also stock up on vegetables that are in season.

Just remember that some vegetables require blanching before dehydrating. Avoid mixing pungent vegetables with those that have milder scents since the circulating air will make these smells stick to the others. You can try carrots, tomatoes, potatoes, celery, mushrooms, corn, chives, cabbage, zucchini, kale, leeks, and more.

Herbs and spices

Store-bought herbs and spices can sometimes be quite expensive. Dehydrate fresh herbs to add to dishes or ground up some seeds to make your own spices. To preserve the natural flavors, oil, and texture, make sure that you don't apply too much heat when dehydrating. 95 degrees F is enough to dehydrate most herbs.

To get the best quality, pick your herbs in the morning just after the dew evaporates. Try drying garlic, onion, basil, mint, chili pepper, oregano, tarragon, cinnamon, and peppercorn.

Meats

Beef jerky from supermarkets is pricey, but if you own a dehydrator, you'll be able to make jerky of any meat you wish. The best meats to dry are those that have little to no fat and are fresh. You may also dehydrate meats that are pre-cooked.

Fish and seafood

Dried fish, shrimp, squid, and shellfish are popular in Asian cuisine. You can stock up on these and add them to soups and dishes to further enhance the taste. Like meats, opt for fish that are low in fat content.

FAQs About Using a Dehydrator

Is it safe to run a dehydrator overnight?

Yes, the food dehydrators have safety features installed like the automatic shut-off and overheating protection.

What foods cannot be dehydrated?

For safety reasons, never dehydrate meat that has fat in it since it will cause spoilage. Avocados and butter are also not good options for they are mostly fat, and do not sit well when dehydrated. The same is true for nuts and grains that have fat in them.

Is it healthy to eat dehydrated food?

Consuming fresh fruits and vegetables are still your best option if you want to get the maximum amount of nutrient. But since fresh produce has a shorter storage life, it is not always the most practical option for some. Fortunately, their dried counterparts are able to retain most of the vitamins, nutrients, and enzymes, so it surely is a great alternative. Although some nutrients are lost while water is taken out, dehydrated food can still preserve most of the needed vitamins better than any other food preservation methods.

How long will my dehydrated produce last?

If properly dehydrated, dried fruits can last up to 5 years, while vegetables last up to 10. However, it's best practice to use up your dried ingredients between 4 months up to a year.

How do I properly store my dried ingredients?

It is imperative that you store your dehydrated food in airtight containers. Sterilized glass mason jars are a great option, but you may use any container as long as it is properly and tightly sealed.

Vacuum sealing is also excellent at prolonging the shelf-life of your dried food. Freezing them further improves its lifespan. Just make sure that you keep them in a cool and dry place away from direct sunlight, moisture, and air.

Can I use my oven to dehydrate instead of buying a new dehydrator?

Although it is possible to dry food items in an oven, kitchen dehydrators are better at maintaining lower temperatures and circulating the hot air.

These are all essential factors to preserve the natural flavor and nutrient of the food. Dehydrators are much more efficient and provide reliable and consistent results than using a traditional oven.

Are dehydrators noisy when operated?

The Food Dehydrator is a surprisingly quiet appliance and does not have any annoying sounds when it is running a cycle.

Do dehydrators really remove any bacteria in the food?

By removing the water content in the food, microorganisms like bacteria can no longer multiply or survive. For raw meats that you are planning to dehydrate, make sure that you apply high heat or about 160 degrees F in the beginning before bringing it down to 145 degrees F.

Can I only dry food in the dehydrator?

Dehydrators are versatile appliances. You don't have to limit your use to edibles alone. Fruits peels and fragrant flowers can be dried up to make potpourri too. Basically, you can safely use items that you would normally sun dry. Some people have used their dehydrators to dry seeds, jewelry, clay, crafts, cake decorations, paper mache, fire starters, and even dog treats.

Does the process of dehydration also increase the sugars in food?

The sugar content remains the same as the fresh fruit, and dehydration does not augment it. Dried ripe fruits will become much sweeter since the water content was eliminated, leaving you with a more concentrated flavor within a smaller mass.

Is there a way to prevent dried food from browning?

Yes. Browning is the natural reaction of some produce to oxidation. Soaking or spraying your cut fruits with a solution of water and either citric acid, ascorbic acid, or sulfites will prevent it from browning during the process. If you don't have access to any of these, try using a solution of 2 quarts of water and ½ cup of lemon juice. Do not use this solution to fragile leafy greens as it will burn its leaves.

CHAPTER 2: MEAT

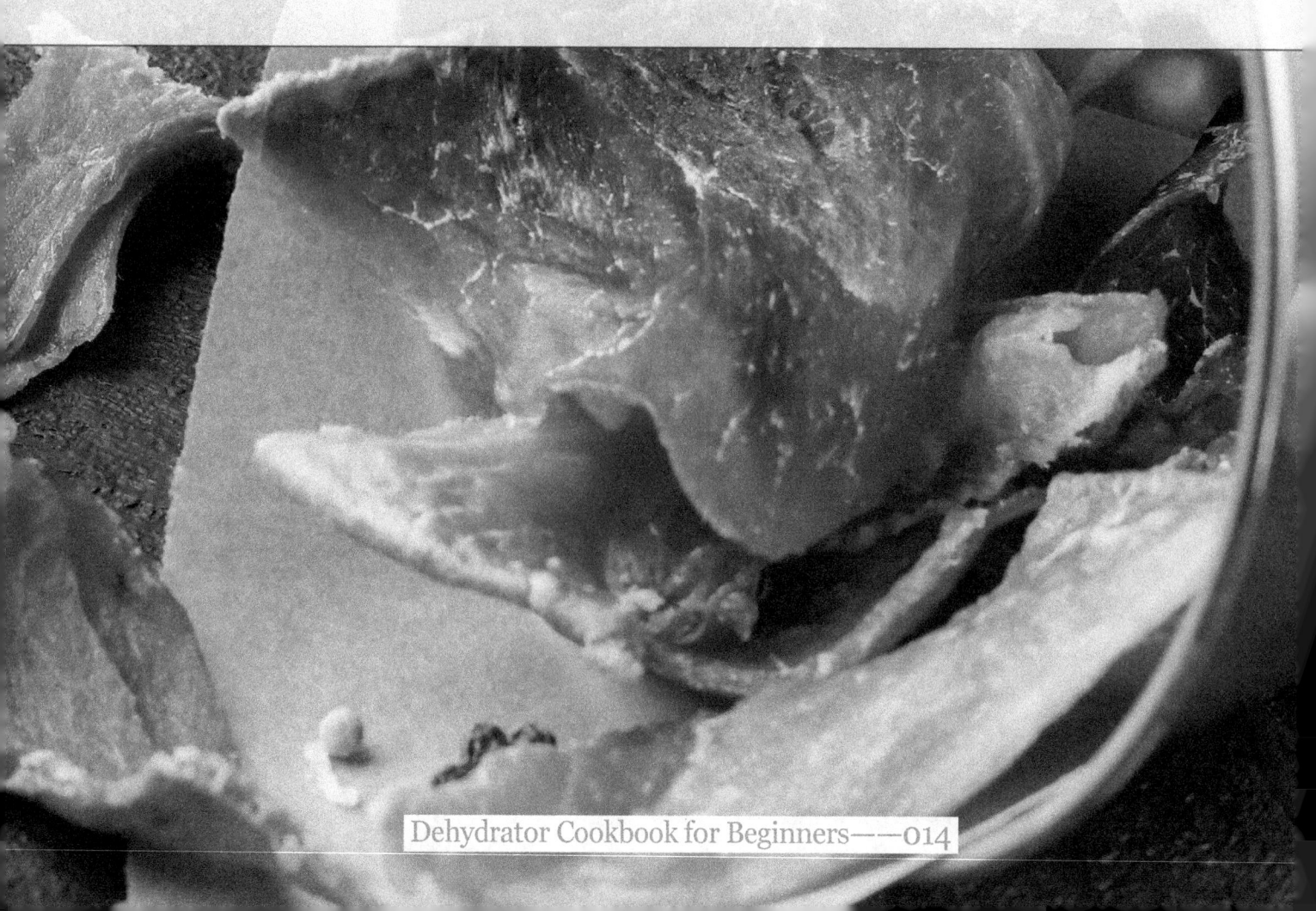

Sweet & Sour Pork

Preparation Time: 12 hours and 10 minutes
Dehydration Time: 6 hours
Servings: 4

Ingredients:

- 1 lb. pork tenderloin, sliced
- 2 tablespoons fish sauce
- ¼ cup lime juice
- ¼ cup brown sugar
- 1 shallot, grated
- 2 garlic cloves, grated
- Salt and pepper to taste

Method:

1. Combine all the ingredients in a bowl.
2. Mix well.
3. Transfer to a sealable plastic bag.
4. Chill in the refrigerator for 12 hours.
5. Remove from the marinade.
6. Transfer the pork slices to the Food Dehydrator.
7. Process at 158 degrees F for 6 hours.

Smoked Herbed Bacon Jerky

Preparation Time: 10 minutes
Dehydration Time: 6 hours
Servings: 4

Ingredients:

- 10 slices smoked bacon
- 1 teaspoon ground fennel seeds
- 1/8 teaspoon onion powder
- 1/8 teaspoon garlic powder
- ¼ teaspoon dried sage
- ¼ teaspoon dried thyme
- 1 teaspoon brown sugar
- ¼ teaspoon red pepper flakes
- 1/8 teaspoon black pepper

Method:

1. Slice the bacon into 3 portions.
2. In a bowl, mix the rest of the ingredients.
3. Sprinkle both sides of the bacon with the seasoning mixture.
4. Add the bacon slices to the Food Dehydrator.
5. Dehydrate at 165 degrees F for 6 hours.

Venison Jerky

Preparation Time: 1 day and 30 minutes
Dehydration Time: 4 hours
Servings: 2

Ingredients:

- 1 lb. venison roast, silver skin trimmed and sliced thinly
- 4 tablespoons coconut amino
- ¼ teaspoon onion powder
- ¼ teaspoon garlic powder
- ¼ teaspoon red pepper flakes
- 1 tablespoon honey
- 4 tablespoons Worcestershire sauce
- Salt and pepper to taste

Method:

1. Place the venison roast slices in a bowl.
2. In another bowl, combine the rest of the ingredients.
3. Pour this mixture into the first bowl.
4. Stir to coat meat evenly with the mixture.
5. Cover the bowl.
6. Chill in the refrigerator for 1 day, stirring every 3 or 4 hours.
7. Drain the marinade.
8. Place the venison slices in the Food Dehydrator.
9. Process at 160 degrees F for 4 hours.

Vietnamese Beef Jerky

Preparation Time: 12 hours and 10 minutes
Dehydration Time: 6 hours
Servings: 4

Ingredients:

- 2 lb. beef round
- 3 tablespoons fish sauce
- 1 tablespoon soy sauce
- 2 tablespoons lime juice
- ¼ cup brown sugar

Method:

1. Combine all the ingredients in a bowl.
2. Transfer to a sealable plastic bag.
3. Turn to coat the beef strips evenly with the marinade.
4. Place in the refrigerator for 12 hours.
5. Drain the marinade.
6. Add the beef to the Food Dehydrator.
7. Process at 165 degrees F for 6 hours.

Paprika Pork Jerky

Preparation Time: 12 hours and 10 minutes
Dehydration Time: 6 hours
Servings: 2

Ingredients:

- 1 lb. pork tenderloin, sliced
- ½ cup ketchup
- 1 teaspoon onion powder
- 1 teaspoon garlic powder
- 1 teaspoon smoked paprika
- 1 teaspoon ground mustard
- 1 teaspoon chili powder
- Salt and pepper to taste

Method:

1. Add the ketchup to a bowl.
2. Stir in the onion powder, garlic powder, paprika, mustard, chili powder, salt and pepper.
3. Mix well.
4. Transfer the mixture to a sealable plastic bag.
5. Add the pork to the plastic bag.
6. Seal and refrigerate for 12 hours.
7. Remove the pork from the marinade.
8. Add to the Food Dehydrator.
9. Dry at 158 degrees F for 6 hours.

Beer Beef Jerky

Preparation Time: 6 hours and 10 minutes
Dehydration Time: 5 hours
Servings: 2

Ingredients:

- 1 lb. beef round, sliced
- ½ cup soy sauce
- 2 cloves garlic, minced
- 2 cups beer
- 1 tablespoon liquid smoke
- 1 tablespoon honey
- Pepper to taste

Method:

1. Add the beef to a sealable plastic bag.
2. Combine the rest of the ingredients in a bowl.
3. Pour the mixture into the bag.
4. Seal and refrigerate for 6 hours.
5. Drain the marinade.
6. Place the beef in the Food Dehydrator.
7. Dehydrate at 160 degrees F for 1 hour.
8. Reduce temperature to 150 degrees F and process for additional 4 hours.

Fish Teriyaki Jerky

Preparation Time: 4 hours and 10 minutes
Dehydration Time: 8 hours
Servings: 2

Ingredients:

- 1 lb. salmon, sliced
- ¼ teaspoon ginger, grated
- ¼ cup sugar
- ½ cup soy sauce
- ¼ cup orange juice
- 1 clove garlic, minced

Method:

1. Combine all the ingredients in a bowl.
2. Mix well.
3. Transfer to a sealable plastic bag.
4. Seal and refrigerate for 4 hours.
5. Drain the marinade.
6. Add the salmon to the Food Dehydrator.
7. Process at 145 degrees F for 8 hours.

Pork Jerky in Chipotle Sauce

Preparation Time: 12 hours and 10 minutes
Dehydration Time: 6 hours
Servings: 2

Ingredients:

- 1 tablespoon tomato paste
- 7 oz. chipotle adobo sauce
- 1 teaspoon salt
- 1 teaspoon sugar
- 1 teaspoon garlic powder
- 1 lb. pork tenderloin, sliced

Method:

1. Mix the tomato paste, chipotle adobo sauce, salt, sugar and garlic powder in a bowl.
2. Transfer to a sealable plastic bag along with the pork tenderloin slices.
3. Seal and refrigerate for 12 hours.
4. Drain the marinade.
5. Add the pork slices to the Food Dehydrator.
6. Process at 158 degrees F for 6 hours.

Beef Teriyaki Jerky

Preparation Time: 12 hours and 10 minutes
Dehydration Time: 6 hours
Servings: 4

Ingredients:

- 2 lb. beef round, sliced
- ¼ cup brown sugar
- ½ cup soy sauce
- ¼ cup pineapple juice
- 1 clove garlic, crushed
- ¼ teaspoon ginger, grated

Method:

1. Add all the ingredients in a bowl.
2. Mix well.
3. Transfer to a sealable plastic bag.
4. Add the beef to the plastic bag.
5. Marinate in the refrigerator for 12 hours.
6. Discard the marinade before dehydrating.
7. Add to the Food Dehydrator.
8. Process at 165 degrees F for 6 hours.

Beef Jerky

Preparation Time: 12 hours and 10 minutes
Dehydration Time: 6 hours
Servings: 4

Ingredients:

- 2 lb. beef eye of round
- ½ cup soy sauce
- ½ cup Worcestershire sauce
- 1 teaspoon salt
- 1 tablespoon honey

Method:

1. Slice the beef eye of round across the grain.
2. Add the soy sauce, Worcestershire sauce, salt and honey in a sealable plastic bag.
3. Add the beef to the plastic bag.
4. Turn to coat.
5. Place inside the refrigerator for 12 hours.
6. Drain the marinade.
7. Add the beef to the Food Dehydrator.
8. Process at 165 degrees F for 6 hours.

Mustard Beef Jerky with Balsamic Vinegar

Preparation Time: 12 hours and 10 minutes
Dehydration Time: 6 hours
Servings: 4

Ingredients:

- 2 lb. beef round, sliced
- 2 tablespoons olive oil
- 1 tablespoon Dijon mustard
- 1 cup balsamic vinegar
- 2 garlic cloves, crushed
- 1 teaspoon salt

Method:

1. Add the beef to a sealable plastic bag.
2. Combine the rest of the ingredients in a bowl.
3. Mix well.
4. Pour the mixture into the plastic bag.
5. Place in the refrigerator for 12 hours.
6. Drain the marinade.
7. Add the beef slices to the Food Dehydrator.
8. Set the dehydrator to 165 degrees F.
9. Dry for 6 hours.

Cajun Fish Jerky

Preparation Time: 4 hours and 10 minutes
Dehydration Time: 8 hours
Servings: 2

Ingredients:

- 1 teaspoon garlic powder
- 1 teaspoon paprika
- 1 teaspoon onion powder
- ¼ teaspoon cayenne pepper
- 1 tablespoon lemon juice
- Salt and pepper to taste
- 1 lb. cod fillet, sliced

Method:

1. Mix the spices, lemon juice, salt and pepper in a bowl.
2. Season the fish with this mixture.
3. Transfer the seasoned fish and marinade in a sealable plastic bag.
4. Marinate in the refrigerator for 4 hours.
5. Drain the marinade.
6. Arrange the salmon slices on the Food Dehydrator.
7. Process at 145 degrees F for 8 hours.

Lamb Jerky

Preparation Time: 13 hours
Dehydration Time: 6 hours
Servings: 4

Ingredients:

- 3 lb. leg of lamb, sliced
- ¼ cup soy sauce
- 3 tablespoons Worcestershire sauce
- 1 tablespoon oregano
- 1 teaspoon garlic powder
- 1 1/2 teaspoons onion powder
- Pepper to taste

Method:

1. Add the lamb slices to a sealable plastic bag.
2. Combine the remaining ingredients in a bowl.
3. Mix well.
4. Pour the mixture into a sealable plastic bag.
5. Marinate in the refrigerator for 13 hours.
6. Place the lamb slices to the Food Dehydrator.
7. Process at 145 degrees F for 6 hours.

Beef Bulgogi Jerky

Preparation Time: 12 hours and 10 minutes
Dehydration Time: 6 hours
Servings: 4

Ingredients:

- 2 lb. beef round, sliced
- 4 tablespoons brown sugar
- 4 tablespoons soy sauce
- 1 tablespoon garlic powder
- 1 tablespoon sesame oil
- Sal to taste

Method:

1. Place the beef inside a sealable plastic bag.
2. In a bowl, mix the remaining ingredients.
3. Add the mixture to the plastic bag.
4. Place the beef in the refrigerator for 12 hours.
5. Drain the marinade.
6. Add the beef to the Food Dehydrator.
7. Set at 165 degrees F.
8. Process for 6 hours.

Candied Bacon

Preparation Time: 12 hours and 10 minutes
Dehydration Time: 6 hours
Servings: 4

Ingredients:

- 10 slices bacon
- 3 tablespoons brown sugar
- 3 tablespoons soy sauce
- 2 teaspoons mirin
- 2 teaspoons sesame oil
- 2 tablespoons chili garlic sauce

Method:

1. Slice each bacon strip into 3 portions.
2. Add the rest of the ingredients in a bowl.
3. Mix well.
4. Add the bacon slices in the mixture.
5. Cover and refrigerate for 12 hours.
6. Add the bacon to the Food Dehydrator.
7. Dehydrate at 165 degrees F for 6 hours.

Buffalo Jerky

Preparation Time: 15 hours and 10 minutes
Dehydration Time: 6 hours
Servings: 4

Ingredients:

- 2 lb. beef round, sliced
- 1 teaspoon salt
- 1 cup buffalo sauce

Method:

1. Season the beef slices with the salt.
2. Add the buffalo sauce to a bowl.
3. Stir in the seasoned beef.
4. Cover the bowl.
5. Refrigerate for 15 hours.
6. Drain the marinade.
7. Add the beef slices to the Food Dehydrator.
8. Process at 165 degrees F for 6 hours.

Salmon Jerky

Preparation Time: 4 hours and 10 minutes
Dehydration Time: 8 hours
Servings: 2

Ingredients:

- 1 ¼ lb. salmon, sliced
- ½ cup soy sauce
- 1 tablespoon molasses
- 1 tablespoon lemon juice
- Pepper to taste

Method:

1. Place the salmon slices in a sealable plastic bag.
2. Combine the rest of the ingredients in a bowl.
3. Add the mixture to the plastic bag.
4. Marinate inside the refrigerator for 4 hours.
5. Drain the marinade.
6. Add the salmon slices to the Food Dehydrator
7. Process at 145 degrees F for 8 hours.

Hickory Smoked Jerky

Preparation Time: 12 hours and 10 minutes
Dehydration Time: 4 hours
Servings: 4

Ingredients:

- 1 lb. beef round, sliced
- ½ cup hickory smoked marinade
- ¼ cup barbecue sauce
- 2 tablespoons brown sugar
- 1 teaspoon onion powder
- Pinch cayenne pepper
- Salt and pepper to taste

Method:

1. Place the beef slices in a sealable plastic bag.
2. In a bowl, combine the marinade, barbecue sauce, sugar, onion powder, cayenne, salt and pepper.
3. Pour the mixture into the bag.
4. Seal and marinate in the refrigerator for 12 hours.
5. Discard the marinade and add the beef to the Food Dehydrator.
6. Process at 180 degrees F for 4 hours, flipping halfway through.

Barbecue Beef Jerky

Preparation Time: 12 hours and 10 minutes
Dehydration Time: 6 hours
Servings: 4

Ingredients:

- 2 lb. beef round, sliced
- Salt and pepper to taste
- 2 teaspoons dried oregano
- 2 teaspoons ground cumin
- 1 teaspoon onion powder
- 1 teaspoon ground coriander
- 4 cloves garlic, grated
- ½ cup olive oil
- ½ cup lime juice
- 1 teaspoon red pepper flakes

Method:

1. Add the beef slices to a sealable plastic bag.
2. In a bowl, mix the salt, pepper, herbs, spices, garlic, olive oil, lime juice and red pepper flakes.
3. Pour mixture into the plastic bag.
4. Turn to coat beef slices evenly with the mixture.
5. Seal and marinate for 12 hours.
6. Drain the marinade.
7. Place the beef slices to the Cosori Food Dehydrator Dehydrator.
8. Set it to 165 degrees F and process for 6 hours.

Lemon Fish Jerky

Preparation Time: 4 hours and 10 minutes
Dehydration Time: 8 hours
Servings: 2

Ingredients:

- 1 lb. cod fillet, sliced
- 1 tablespoon lemon juice
- 1 teaspoon lemon zest
- 2 tablespoons olive oil
- 1 teaspoon dill
- 1 clove garlic, grated
- Salt to taste

Method:

1. Combine the fish slices and the rest of the ingredients in a sealable plastic bag.
2. Turn to coat the fish evenly with the marinade.
3. Place the plastic bag inside the refrigerator for 4 hours.
4. Drain the marinade.
5. Add the fish slices to the Food Dehydrator.
6. Process at 145 degrees F for 8 hours.

CHAPTER 3: FRUITS

Plum & Grape Fruit Leather

Preparation Time: 20 minutes
Dehydration Time: 12 hours
Servings: 4

Ingredients:

- 2 cups red grapes (seedless)
- 5 plums, sliced
- 2 tablespoons sugar

Method:

1. Put all the ingredients in a pot over medium low heat.
2. Cook for 15 minutes.
3. Transfer the mixture to a blender.
4. Blend until smooth.
5. Pour the mixture into a fruit roll sheet.
6. Place in the Food Dehydrator.
7. Process at 165 degrees F for 12 hours.

Blackberry & Blueberry Fruit Rolls

Preparation Time: 10 minutes
Dehydration Time: 9 hours
Servings: 4

Ingredients:

- 1 lb. blueberries
- 1 cup blackberries

Method:

1. Add the berries to a blender.
2. Blend on low speed until fully combined.
3. Strain the mixture and remove the seeds.
4. Put the mixture back to the blender.
5. Pulse until the mixture has turned into liquid.
6. Pour the mixture into a fruit roll sheet and place in the Food Dehydrator.
7. Process at 165 degrees F for 9 hours.

Raspberry Rolls

Preparation Time: 10 minutes
Dehydration Time: 5 hours
Servings: 4

Ingredients:

- 1 ½ lb. raspberries
- 2 tablespoons sugar

Method:

1. Add the raspberries and sugars to a blender.
2. Blend until smooth.
3. Strain to remove the seeds.
4. Add the pureed raspberry back to the blender.
5. Blend until the mixture has turned into liquid.
6. Add the liquid to a fruit roll sheet.
7. Place these in the Food Dehydrator.
8. Dehydrate at 165 degrees F for 5 hours.

Choco Bananas

Preparation Time: 15 minutes
Dehydration Time: 16 hours
Servings: 2

Ingredients:

- 1 banana, sliced thinly
- 4 oz. chocolate chips
- Sea salt

Method:

1. Arrange the banana slices in the Food Dehydrator.
2. Process at 145 degrees F for 16 hours.
3. In a pan over medium low heat, melt the chocolate for 5 to 10 minutes.
4. Dip the dried bananas in the chocolate.
5. Sprinkle with the sea salt.

Berry Fruit Leather

Preparation Time: 10 minutes
Dehydration Time: 10 hours
Servings: 4

Ingredients:

- 1 lb. strawberries
- ½ cup raspberries
- 1 teaspoon vanilla extract

Method:

1. Process all the ingredients in a blender.
2. Pulse until smooth.
3. Strain to remove seeds.
4. Put the mixture back to the blender.
5. Pulse until liquified.
6. Pour the fruit puree into a fruit roll sheet and place in the Food Dehydrator.
7. Dehydrate at 165 degrees F for 10 hours.

Dried Apple Chips with Cinnamon

Preparation Time: 15 hours
Dehydration Time: 10 hours
Servings: 2

Ingredients:

- 2 apples, sliced
- 1 tablespoon lemon juice
- 2 teaspoons cinnamon powder

Method:

1. Drizzle the apple slices with lemon juice.
2. Arrange the apple slices in the Food Dehydrator.
3. Process at 135 degrees F for 10 hours.
4. Sprinkle with the cinnamon before serving.

Candied Pumpkin

Preparation Time: 15 minutes
Dehydration Time: 8 hours
Servings: 2

Ingredients:

- 1 cup coconut milk
- 2 cups applesauce
- 2 cups pumpkin puree
- ¼ cup honey
- ½ teaspoon ground allspice
- ½ teaspoon ground nutmeg
- 1 teaspoon ground cinnamon
- ¼ cup coconut flakes
- 2 tablespoons dried cranberries, chopped

Method:

1. Combine all the ingredients in a bowl.
2. Spread the mixture in the fruit leather sheet of your Food Dehydrator.
3. Dehydrate at 135 degrees F for 8 hours.

Cinnamon Apple Chips

Preparation Time: 10 minutes
Dehydration Time: 12 hours
Servings: 4

Ingredients:

- 2 apples, sliced thinly
- 1 tablespoon white sugar
- 1 tablespoon lemon juice
- ¼ teaspoon nutmeg
- ½ teaspoon vanilla extract
- 1 teaspoon ground cinnamon

Method:

1. Combine all the ingredients in a bowl.
2. Coat the apples slices evenly with the mixture.
3. Arrange the apple slices in the Food Dehydrator.
4. Dehydrate at 145 degrees F for 6 hours.

Dried Mangoes

Preparation Time: 15 minutes
Dehydration Time: 12 hours
Servings: 2

Ingredients:

- 2 mangoes, sliced thinly
- 2 tablespoons honey
- 3 teaspoons lemon juice

Method:

1. Marinate the mangoes in honey and lemon juice for 15 minutes.
2. Transfer mango slices in the Food Dehydrator.
3. Dry at 165 degrees F for 12 hours.

Fruit Leather

Preparation Time: 30 minutes
Dehydration Time: 8 hours
Servings: 4

Ingredients:

- 3 peaches, sliced
- 3 apricots, sliced
- 1 tablespoon sugar

Method:

1. Put the peaches and apricots in a pot over medium low heat.
2. Sprinkle with sugar.
3. Mix well.
4. Cook for 10 minutes.
5. Let cool.
6. Transfer to a blender.
7. Blend on low speed until pureed.
8. Pour the mixture into a fruit roll sheet.
9. Place the roll sheet in the Food Dehydrator.
10. Dehydrate at 165 degrees F or 8 hours.

Blackberry Tuile

Preparation Time: 10 minutes
Dehydration Time: 3 hours
Servings: 4

Ingredients:

- 1 ½ lb. blackberries
- 2 tablespoons white sugar

Method:

1. Process the blackberries and sugar in a blender.
2. Strain the mixture to remove the seeds.
3. Add the mixture to the blender.
4. Process on high speed.
5. Pour the fruit liquid into a fruit roll sheet.
6. Place these in the Food Dehydrator.
7. Dehydrate at 165 degrees F for 3 hours.

Dried Kiwi

Preparation Time: 15 minutes
Dehydration Time: 12 hours
Servings: 2

Ingredients:

- 2 kiwis, peeled and sliced thinly

Method:

1. Place the kiwi slices in the Food Dehydrator.
2. Dry at 135 degrees F for 12 hours.

Honey Peaches with Bourbon

Preparation Time: 4 hours and 10 minutes
Dehydration Time: 16 hours
Servings: 1

Ingredients:

- 1 peach, cored and sliced
- ¼ cup honey
- ¼ cup hot water
- 3 tablespoons bourbon

Method:

1. Add the slices to a sealable plastic bag.
2. In a glass bowl, mix the honey and hot water.
3. Mix until the honey has been dissolved.
4. Pour in the bourbon.
5. Let cool.
6. Once cool, add this to the plastic bag.
7. Marinate for 4 hours.
8. Drain the marinade.
9. Add these to the Food Dehydrator.
10. Dehydrate at 145 degrees F for 16 hours.

Dried Papaya Cubes

Preparation Time: 10 minutes
Dehydration Time: 12 hours
Servings: 4

Ingredients:

- 2 papaya, diced

Method:

1. Add the diced papaya to the Food Dehydrator.
2. Process at 135 degrees F for 12 hours.

Apple Fruit Leather

Preparation Time: 10 minutes
Dehydration Time: 6 hours
Servings: 2

Ingredients:

- 2 cups applesauce
- 2 cups sweet potatoes, cooked and mashed
- ¼ cup honey
- 1 teaspoon cinnamon
- Salt to taste

Method:

1. Add all the ingredients to a blender.
2. Pulse until smooth.
3. Add the mixture to fruit roll sheets and place in the Food Dehydrator.
4. Dry at 100 degrees F for 6 hours.

Peanut Butter & Banana Leather

Preparation Time: 5 minutes
Dehydration Time: 4 hours
Servings: 2

Ingredients:

- 2 bananas, sliced
- 2 tablespoons peanut butter

Method:

1. Process bananas and peanut butter in a food processor for 1 minute.
2. Spread a layer of the mixture onto the dehydrator sheet.
3. Dry at 135 degrees F for 4 hours.

Hazelnut Banana Leather

Preparation Time: 5 minutes
Dehydration Time: 3 hours
Servings: 2

Ingredients:

- 2 bananas, sliced
- Chocolate hazelnut spread

Method:

1. Combine the bananas and chocolate hazelnut spread in your food processor.
2. Pulse until smooth.
3. Form round shapes of about ¼ inch thick on parchment paper.
4. Transfer to the Food Dehydrator.
5. Process at 125 degrees F for 4 hours.

Dried Lemon

Preparation Time: 5 minutes
Dehydration Time: 10 hours
Servings: 2

Ingredients:

- 2 lemons, sliced

Method:

1.Arrange the lemon slices in the Food Dehydrator.
2.Dry the lemon at 125 degrees F for 10 hours.

Dried Strawberries

Preparation Time: 10 minutes
Dehydration Time: 8 hours
Servings: 4

Ingredients:

- 1 lb. strawberries, sliced

Method:

1. Place the strawberry slices in the Food Dehydrator.
2. Process at 135 degrees F for 8 hours.

Orange Fruit Leather

Preparation Time: 10 minutes
Dehydration Time: 6 hours
Servings: 4

Ingredients:

- 1 cup applesauce
- 1 cup orange juice concentrate
- 32 oz. vanilla yogurt

Method:

1. Add all the ingredients in your blender.
2. Pulse until smooth.
3. Spread the mixture onto the roll sheet.
4. Dry at 135 degrees F for 6 hours.

CHAPTER 4: VEGETABLES

Dried Sweet Potato

Preparation Time: 10 minutes
Dehydration Time: 12 hours
Servings: 4

Ingredients:

- 2 sweet potatoes
- 1 teaspoon onion powder

Method:

1. Season the sweet potato slices with onion powder.
2. Arrange in a single layer in the Food Dehydrator.
3. Set at 115 degrees F.
4. Process for 12 hours.

Broccoli & Cashew Bites

Preparation Time: 15 minutes
Dehydration Time: 4 hours
Servings: 12

Ingredients:

- 2 ½ cups broccoli florets
- 2 ½ cups cashews
- ¼ cup onion, chopped
- 3 cloves garlic, crushed and minced
- 2 tablespoons olive oil
- 1 tablespoon jalapeno, chopped
- ¼ cup nutritional yeast
- Salt to taste

Method:

1. Add the broccoli and cashews to a blender or food processor.
2. Pulse until powdery.
3. Stir in the rest of the ingredients.
4. Pulse until smooth.
5. Form balls from the mixture.
6. Add these to the Food Dehydrator.
7. Dry at 115 degrees F for 4 hours.

Paprika Zucchini

Preparation Time: 10 minutes
Dehydration Time: 12 hours
Servings: 4

Ingredients:

- 2 zucchinis, sliced into rounds
- 1 tablespoon olive oil
- 1 teaspoon onion powder
- 1 teaspoon garlic powder
- 1 teaspoon paprika
- Salt and pepper to taste

Method:

1. Toss the zucchini in olive oil.
2. In another bowl, mix the onion powder, garlic powder, paprika, salt and pepper.
3. Add the zucchini to the Food Dehydrator.
4. Dehydrate at 165 degrees F for 12 hours.

Crunchy Green Peas

Preparation Time: 10 minutes
Dehydration Time: 8 hours
Servings: 4

Ingredients:

- 2 cups green peas, rinsed and drained
- 1 teaspoon olive oil
- Salt to taste

Method:

1. Dry the green peas with paper towels.
2. Add the green peas to a bowl.
3. Coat with oil.
4. Spread in the Food Dehydrator.
5. Dry at 135 degrees F for 8 hours.
6. Sprinkle with salt before storing.

Maple Carrot Straws

Preparation Time: 15 minutes
Dehydration Time: 6 hours
Servings: 4

Ingredients:

- 1 lb. carrots, sliced into long strips
- 1 tablespoon maple syrup
- 1 tablespoon olive oil
- Salt to taste

Method:

1. Combine all the ingredients in a bowl.
2. Arrange the strips in the Food Dehydrator.
3. Process at 135 degrees F for 6 hours.

Cucumber Chips

Preparation Time: 15 minutes
Dehydration Time: 10 hours
Servings: 6

Ingredients:

- 3 cucumber, sliced into rounds
- 1 tablespoon avocado oil
- 2 teaspoons apple cider vinegar
- Salt to taste

Method:

1. Toss the cucumber slices in avocado oil and vinegar.
2. Season with the salt.
3. Add the cucumber slices to the Food Dehydrator.
4. Dehydrate at 135 degrees F for 10 hours.

Dehydrated Asparagus

Preparation Time: 10 minutes
Dehydration Time: 6 hours
Servings: 2

Ingredients:

- 4 cups asparagus, trimmed and sliced

Method:

1. Arrange the asparagus in the Food Dehydrator.
2. Process at 125 degrees F for 6 hours.

Lemon Kale

Preparation Time: 15 minutes
Dehydration Time: 8 hours
Servings: 2

Ingredients:

- 2 cups kale leaves
- 1 tablespoon olive oil
- Salt to taste
- 1 teaspoon lemon juice

Method:

1. Toss the kale leaves in olive oil.
2. Season with the salt.
3. Arrange the kale leaves in the Food Dehydrator.
4. Process at 135 degrees F for 8 hours.
5. Drizzle with lemon juice.

Shawarma Kale

Preparation Time: 15 minutes
Dehydration Time: 13 hours
Servings: 4

Ingredients:

- 4 oz. kale, sliced
- 2 teaspoons olive oil
- Salt to taste
- 1 teaspoon cumin
- ¼ teaspoon ground cardamom
- ½ teaspoon smoked paprika
- ½ teaspoon ground coriander
- ½ teaspoon garlic powder
- ½ teaspoon cinnamon

Method:

1. Toss the kale in olive oil.
2. Stir in the salt and spices.
3. Arrange the kale in the Food Dehydrator.
4. Dehydrate at 135 degrees F for 12 hours.

Spicy Garlic Kale

Preparation Time: 10 minutes
Dehydration Time: 6 hours
Servings: 4

Ingredients:

- 4 cups kale leaves, rinsed
- 2 tablespoons olive oil
- 1 tablespoon dried Sriracha
- ¼ teaspoon garlic powder
- Salt to taste

Method:

1. Arrange the kale leaves in the Food Dehydrator.
2. Dry at 135 degrees F for 6 hours.
3. Toss in the olive oil.
4. Sprinkle with the remaining ingredients.

Spiced Cucumbers

Preparation Time: 20 hours
Dehydration Time: 4 hours
Servings: 2

Ingredients:

- 2 cucumbers, sliced into rounds
- 2 teaspoons olive oil
- 2 teaspoons vinegar
- 1 tablespoon paprika
- 2 teaspoons onion powder
- 2 teaspoons garlic powder
- 2 teaspoons sugar
- Pinch chili powder

Method:

- Toss the cucumbers in oil and vinegar.
- Sprinkle with the sugar and spices.
- Put the cucumber slices in the Food Dehydrator.
- Process at 135 degrees F for 6 hours.

Zucchini Snacks

Preparation Time: 45 minutes
Dehydration Time: 12 hours
Servings: 4

Ingredients:

- 8 zucchinis, sliced into rounds and seeds removed
- 1 cup grape juice concentrate
- 1 cup water

Method:

1. Add all the ingredients to a pot over medium heat.
2. Bring to a boil.
3. Reduce heat and simmer for 30 minutes.
4. Drain the zucchini and let cool.
5. Add the zucchinis to the Food Dehydrator.
6. Process at 135 degrees F for 12 hours.

Dehydrated Okra

Preparation Time: 15 minutes
Dehydration Time: 12 hours
Servings: 4

Ingredients:

- 12 okra, sliced

Method:

1. Add the okra to the Food Dehydrator.
2. Dry at 130 degrees F for 12 hours.

Green Bean Crisps

Preparation Time: 10 minutes
Dehydration Time: 6 hours
Servings: 5

Ingredients:

- 2 lb. green beans
- 1 teaspoons olive oil
- Salt to taste

Method:

1. Coat the green beans with oil.
2. Sprinkle with the salt.
3. Spread it in the Food Dehydrator.
4. Dehydrate at 115 degrees F for 6 hours.

Dehydrated Tomatoes

Preparation Time: 20 minutes
Dehydration Time: 8 hours
Servings: 2

Ingredients:

- 2 tomatoes, sliced into quarters
- Salt to taste

Method:

1. Add the tomatoes to the Food Dehydrator.
2. Sprinkle with salt.
3. Set to 135 degrees F.
4. Process for 8 hours.

Dehydrated Pizza Broccoli

Preparation Time: 15 minutes
Dehydration Time: 16 hours
Servings: 6

Ingredients:

- 3 cups broccoli florets
- 2 tomatoes, sliced in half
- 1 tablespoon dried basil
- 1 tablespoon dried oregano
- 2 cloves garlic, minced
- ¼ yellow onion, chopped
- 1 tablespoon smoked paprika
- 2 tablespoons tahini

Method:

1. Add all the broccoli florets to a bowl.
2. Blend the remaining ingredients in a food processor.
3. Pulse until smooth.
4. Toss the broccoli florets in the sauce.
5. Arrange the broccoli florets in the Food Dehydrator.
6. Process at 135 degrees F for 16 hours.

Dehydrated Corn

Preparation Time: 10 minutes
Dehydration Time: 12 hours
Servings: 4

Ingredients:

- 8 cups corn kernels

Method:

1. Spread the corn kernels in the Food Dehydrator.
2. Process at 125 degrees F for 12 hours.

Dehydrated Beets

Preparation Time: 20 minutes
Dehydration Time: 12 hours
Servings: 4

Ingredients:

- 3 beets, sliced thinly
- ¼ cup water
- ¼ cup vinegar
- 1 tablespoon olive oil
- Salt to taste

Method:

1. Combine all the ingredients in a bowl.
2. Marinate for 10 minutes.
3. Arrange the beet slices in the Food Dehydrator.
4. Dehydrate at 135 degrees F for 12 hours.

Dried Cauliflower Popcorn

Preparation Time: 15 minutes
Dehydration Time: 8 hours
Servings: 1

Ingredients:

- 2 cups cauliflower florets
- 4 tablespoons hot sauce
- 3 tablespoons coconut oil
- 1 teaspoon smoked cayenne
- ½ teaspoon ground cumin
- 1 tablespoons paprika

Method:

1. Toss the cauliflower florets in hot sauce and coconut oil.
2. Sprinkle with the smoked cayenne, cumin and paprika.
3. Add the seasoned cauliflower to the Food Dehydrator.
4. Dry at 130 degrees F for 8 hours.

Ranch Carrot

Preparation Time: 15 minutes
Dehydration Time: 12 hours
Servings: 6

Ingredients:

- 3 cups carrot strips
- 2 tablespoons water
- 1 packet ranch dressing seasoning powder

Method:

1. Soak the carrots in water.
2. Sprinkle with the ranch dressing seasoning.
3. Add the carrots to the Food Dehydrator.
4. Dehydrate at 145 degrees F for 12 hours.

CHAPTER 5: HERBS & POWDER

Tomato Powder

Preparation Time: 15 minutes
Dehydration Time: 12 hours
Servings: 10 to 15

Ingredients:

- Skins from 10 tomatoes

Method:

1. Add the tomato skins to a Food Dehydrator.
2. Dry at 135 degrees F for 12 hours.
3. Transfer the dried tomatoes to a coffee grinder.
4. Grind until the mixture turns to powder.

Onion Powder

Preparation Time: 10 minutes
Dehydration Time: 8 hours
Servings: 10 to 15

Ingredients:

- 5 onions, sliced

Method:

1. Arrange the onion slices in a single layer in the Food Dehydrator.
2. Dehydrate at 145 degrees F for 8 hours.
3. Transfer the dried onion to a food processor.
4. Pulse until powdery.

Powdered Ginger

Preparation Time: 15 minutes
Dehydration Time: 8 hours
Servings: 10 to 15

Ingredients:

- 5 pieces ginger, sliced

Method:

1. Put the ginger in the Food Dehydrator.
2. Dry at 95 degrees F for 8 hours.
3. Transfer the dried ginger to a food processor or spice grinder.
4. Grind the dried ginger into powder.

Dried Parsley, Basil & Oregano Powder

Preparation Time: 15 minutes
Dehydration Time: 8 hours
Servings: 10 to 15

Ingredients:

- 2 tablespoons parsley leaves
- 2 tablespoons basil leaves
- 2 tablespoons oregano leaves
- 2 tablespoons brown sugar
- 2 tablespoons salt

Method:

1. Add the herb leaves to the Food Dehydrator.
2. Dehydrate at 135 degrees F for 8 hours.
3. Transfer the dried leaves to a food processor.
4. Stir in the sugar and salt.

Mushroom Powder

Preparation Time: 15 minutes
Dehydration Time: 12 hours
Servings: 15

Ingredients:

- 2 cups shiitake mushrooms

Method:

1. Arrange the shiitake mushrooms in a single layer in the Food Dehydrator.
2. Dry at 135 degrees F for 12 hours.
3. Place the dried mushrooms in a food processor.
4. Pulse until powdered.

Dried Herb Mix

Preparation Time: 15 minutes
Dehydration Time: 8 hours
Servings: 10 to 15

Ingredients:

- ½ cup thyme leaves
- ½ cup rosemary leaves
- 2 teaspoons lemon zest
- 6 cloves garlic, peeled

Method:

1. Combine all the ingredients in a food processor.
2. Pulse until smooth.
3. Spread the mixture in the Food Dehydrator.
4. Dehydrate at 135 degrees F for 8 hours.

Thyme, Garlic, Rosemary & Lemon Herb Mix

Preparation Time: 15 minutes
Dehydration Time: 8 hours
Servings: 15

Ingredients:

- ½ cup thyme leaves
- 6 cloves garlic, peeled
- ½ cup rosemary leaves
- 2 teaspoons lemon zest

Method:

1. Add all the ingredients to a food processor.
2. Pulse until well mixed.
3. Add the mixture to the Food Dehydrator.
4. Dry at 135 degrees F for 8 hours.

Taco Seasoning

Preparation Time: 15 minutes
Dehydration Time: 12 hours
Servings: 15

Ingredients:

- 1 cup oregano leaves
- 2 tablespoons ground cumin
- 2 tablespoons cayenne pepper
- 1 tablespoon onion powder
- 1 tablespoon garlic powder
- 1 tablespoon sweet paprika
- ½ teaspoon black pepper

Method:

1. Add the oregano leaves to the Food Dehydrator.
2. Dehydrate at 145 degrees F for 12 hours.
3. Add to the spice grinder.
4. Grind until powdered.
5. Add the oregano powder in a glass jar.
6. Stir in the rest of the ingredients.
7. Shake to blend well.

Onion & Garlic Powder Mix

Preparation Time: 20 minutes
Dehydration Time: 12 hours
Servings:

Ingredients:

- 5 cloves garlic, peeled and sliced
- 1 onion, sliced

Method:

1. Place the garlic and onion slices in the Food Dehydrator.
2. Dehydrate at 135 degrees F for 12 hours.
3. Transfer to a spice grinder.
4. Grind until powdery.

Dried Herbs For Salad

Preparation Time: 15 minutes
Dehydration Time: 12 hours
Servings: 15

Ingredients:

- 1 cup parsley leaves
- ½ cup basil leaves
- ½ cup Parmesan cheese, grated
- 2 teaspoons paprika
- 2 teaspoons onion powder
- 2 teaspoons garlic powder
- Salt and pepper to taste

Method:

1. Place the parsley and basil leaves in the Food Dehydrator.
2. Process at 145 degrees F for 12 hours.
3. Transfer to the spice grinder.

Kimchi Powder

Preparation Time: 5 minutes
Dehydration Time: 12 hours
Servings: 5

Ingredients:

- 2 cups kimchi

Method:

1. Add the kimchi to the Food Dehydrator.
2. Dehydrate at 155 degrees F for 12 hours.
3. Add the dried kimchi to a spice grinder, blender or food processor.
4. Process until powdery.

Herbes de Provence

Preparation Time: 15 minutes
Dehydration Time: 8 hours
Servings: 15

Ingredients:

- 1 cup fresh basil leaves
- 1 cup fresh marjoram leaves
- 1 cup fresh rosemary leaves
- ½ cup fresh tarragon leaves
- ½ cup fresh thyme leaves
- ½ cup lavender buds
- 2 tablespoons dried savory

Method:

1. Add the fresh herbs to the Food Dehydrator by batch. Do not overcrowd.
2. Dehydrate at 145 degrees F for 8 hours.
3. Transfer dried herbs to a food processor or spice grinder.
4. Grind until powdered.

Parsley, Oregano, Basil, Thyme & Red Pepper Herb Mix

Preparation Time: 15 minutes
Dehydration Time: 8 hours
Servings: 15

Ingredients:

- 2 tablespoons fresh oregano leaves
- 2 tablespoons fresh parsley leaves
- 2 tablespoons fresh basil leaves
- 1 tablespoon fresh thyme leaves
- 1 teaspoon lemon zest
- 1 teaspoon red pepper, sliced

Method:

1. Combine all the ingredients in a bowl.
2. Add to the Food Dehydrator.
3. Dehydrate at 135 degrees F for 8 hours.
4. After dehydrating the herbs and spices, transfer to a food processor.
5. Pulse until powdery.

Garlic Powder

Preparation Time: 15 minutes
Dehydration Time: 12 hours
Servings: 24

Ingredients:

- 6 heads garlic, cloves separated, peeled and sliced

Method:

1. Spread the garlic slices in the Food Dehydrator.
2. Dry at 125 degrees F for 12 hours.
3. Transfer the dried garlic into a blender or spice grinder.

Lemon Powder

Preparation Time: 30 minutes
Dehydration Time: 12 hours
Servings: 15

Ingredients:

- Peel from 6 lemons

Method:

1. Add the lemon peels to the Food Dehydrator.
2. Dehydrate at 95 degrees F for 12 hours.
3. Transfer to a food processor.
4. Pulse until powdered.

Dried Basil Powder

Preparation Time: 10 minutes
Dehydration Time: 15 hours
Servings: 10 to 15

Ingredients:

- 3 cups basil leaves

Method:

1. Add the basil leaves to the Food Dehydrator.
2. Dry at 105 degrees for 15 hours.
3. Grind the dried basil in a spice grinder or food processor.

Leek Powder

Preparation Time: 5 minutes
Dehydration Time: 12 hours
Servings: 10 to 15

Ingredients:

- 4 cups leeks, sliced

Method:

1. Place the leeks in the Food Dehydrator.
2. Dehydrate at 135 degrees F for 4 hours.
3. Put the dried leeks in a spice grinder.
4. Grind until powdery.

Italian Seasoning Blend

Preparation Time: 15 minutes
Dehydration Time: 8 hours
Servings: 15

Ingredients:

- 1 cup fresh oregano leaves
- 1 cup fresh basil leaves
- 1 cup fresh thyme leaves
- ½ cup fresh sage leaves
- ½ cup fresh rosemary leaves

Method:

1. Arrange the fresh herb leaves in the Food Dehydrator by batch.
2. Dehydrate at 145 degrees F for 8 hours.
3. Put the dried herbs in a food processor.
4. Pulse until powdered.

Basil, Marjoram & Sage Herb Mix

Preparation Time: 15 minutes
Dehydration Time: 12 hours
Servings: 15

Ingredients:

- 1 cup fresh basil leaves
- 1 cup fresh marjoram leaves
- 1 cup fresh sage leaves

Method:

1. Place the fresh herbs in the Food Dehydrator.
2. Dehydrate at 145 degrees F for 12 hours.
3. Transfer to a spice grinder.
4. Grind until powdered.

Porcini Cubes

Preparation Time: 20 minutes
Dehydration Time: 10 hours
Servings: 15

Ingredients:

- 2 oz. dried porcini mushrooms
- 2 teaspoons gelatin powder
- 3 tablespoons onion powder
- 2 tablespoons soy sauce
- 1 teaspoon fish sauce
- 1 tablespoon water
- 2 teaspoons salt

Method:

1. Combine all the ingredients in a bowl.
2. Form small balls from the mixture.
3. Shape into cubes.
4. Add the cubes to the Food Dehydrator.
5. Dry at 125 degrees F for 10 hours.

CHAPTER 6: CRACKERS

Carrot Crackers

Preparation Time: 20 minutes
Dehydration Time: 10 hours
Servings: 10

Ingredients:

- 1 cup almonds, soaked overnight, rinsed, and drained
- 2 cups carrot pulp
- 1 tablespoon ground chia seeds
- 2 tablespoons ground flax seed
- 1 teaspoon Italian seasoning
- 1 tablespoon coconut aminos
- ½ teaspoon smoked paprika
- 1 tablespoon dried onion
- ½ teaspoon red pepper flakes
- 2 cups water

Method:

1. Add the almonds to a food processor or blender.
2. Pulse until crumbly.
3. Stir in the rest of the ingredients.
4. Pulse until fully combined.
5. Spread a thin layer of the dough in the Food Dehydrator.
6. Dry at 125 degrees F for 2 hours.
7. Score the dough to form the crackers.
Dry at 115 degrees for 8 hours.

Sesame & Carrot Crackers

Preparation Time: 45 minutes
Dehydration Time: 24 hours
Servings: 15

Ingredients:

- 1 ½ cups of golden flaxseeds
- ¼ cup sesame seeds
- 2 cups carrot pulp
- 1 teaspoon of garlic powder
- ½ teaspoon of ground coriander
- 3 tablespoons tamari
- 1 cup water

Method:

1. Grind the flaxseeds in the spice grinder.
2. Add to a bowl along with the remaining ingredients.
3. Mix well.
4. Let sit for 30 minutes.
5. Spread the mixture in the Food Dehydrator.
6. Process at 110 degrees F for 24 hours.

Green Crackers

Preparation Time: 20 minutes
Dehydration Time: 8 hours
Servings: 6

Ingredients:

- 1 cup green juice pulp
- ¼ cup ground flax seeds
- ¼ cup chia seeds
- ¼ cup nutritional yeast
- 2 tablespoons sesame seeds
- 1 tablespoon tamari
- ½ teaspoon salt
- ¼ cup water

Method:

1. Combine all the ingredients in a bowl.
2. Transfer to a food processor.
3. Pulse until fully combined.
4. Spread a thin layer of the mixture in the Food Dehydrator.
5. Score the crackers.
6. Process at 115 degrees F for 5 hours.
7. Flip the crackers.
8. Dry for another 3 hours.

Mexican Crackers

Preparation Time: 30 minutes
Dehydration Time: X hours
Servings: 15

Ingredients:

- ½ cup chia seeds
- 1 cup golden flaxseeds
- ½ cup pumpkin seeds
- ½ cup sunflower seeds
- 1 red bell pepper, chopped
- ¼ onion, chopped
- 1 cup carrot pulp
- 1 ½ teaspoons chipotle powder
- 1 teaspoon garlic powder
- Salt to taste
- ½ teaspoon cayenne pepper

Method:

1. Process the seeds in a blender or food processor until powdery.
2. Stir in the bell pepper and onion.
3. Pulse until smooth.
4. Stir in the rest of the ingredients.
5. Pulse until fully combined.
6. Spread the mixture in the Food Dehydrator.
7. Score the crackers.
8. Dry at 115 degrees F for 6 hours.

Peanut Butter & Banana Crackers

Preparation Time: 4 hours and 20 minutes
Dehydration Time: 6 hours
Servings: 12

Ingredients:

- 3 bananas, sliced
- ½ cup peanut butter
- ½ teaspoon cinnamon powder
- 1 cup ground peanuts
- 3 cups graham cracker crumbs

Method:

1. Mash the bananas and peanut butter in a bowl.
2. Stir in the rest of the ingredients.
3. Roll the dough into a large ball.
4. Flatten the ball to form a long rectangle.
5. Wrap the dough with wax paper and refrigerate for 4 hours.
6. Roll out the dough and slice.
7. Add the slices to the Food Dehydrator.
8. Process at 145 degrees F for 6 hours.

Flax Crackers

Preparation Time: 4 hours and 10 minutes
Dehydration Time: 24 hours
Servings: 12 crackers

Ingredients:

- 1 ½ cups water
- 1 clove garlic, minced
- ¾ cup golden flax seeds
- ¼ cup flax seeds
- 3 teaspoons sesame seeds, crushed
- 3 teaspoons poppy seeds, crushed
- 3 teaspoons garlic flakes
- 3 teaspoons onion flakes
- 3 teaspoons salt

Method:

1. Add the water and garlic in a blender.
2. Blend until smooth.
3. Pour the mixture in a bowl with the flaxseeds.
4. Soak for 4 hours.
5. Spread the gelatin mixture in the Food Dehydrator.
6. Score the crackers with a knife.
7. Combine the remaining ingredients in a bowl.
8. Sprinkle the mixture on top of the crackers.
9. Process at 110 degrees F for 24 hours.

Seaweed & Tamari Crackers

Preparation Time: 15 minutes
Dehydration Time: 24 hours
Servings: 15

Ingredients:

- 1 cup flax seeds
- 2 nori sheets, broken
- 2 tablespoons tamari
- 1 ½ cups water

Method:

1. Mix all the ingredients in a bowl.
2. Spread a layer in the Food Dehydrator.
3. Set it at 110 degrees F.
4. Process for 24 hours.
5. Break into crackers.

Onion & Nut Crackers

Preparation Time: 15 minutes
Dehydration Time: 12 hours
Servings: 12

Ingredients:

- 1 cup cashews
- 1 cup sunflower seeds
- ¼ cup coconut amino
- ½ cup water
- 1 clove garlic
- 1 green onion, chopped

Method:

1. Pulse all the ingredients in a food processor until fully combined.
2. Spread the mixture in the Food Dehydrator.
3. Dehydrate at 115 degrees F for 1 hour.
4. Score the crackers.
5. Reduce temperature to 105 degrees F and process for another 11 hours.

Seed Crackers

Preparation Time: X hours
Dehydration Time: X hours
Servings: 10

Ingredients:

- ¼ cup chia seeds
- ¾ cup flax seeds
- 1 cup water
- ¼ cup hemp seeds
- 1/3 cup sunflower seeds
- 2 tablespoons pumpkin seeds
- 1 tablespoon Italian seasoning
- Salt and pepper to taste

Method:

1. Soak the chia seeds and flax seeds in water for 1 hour.
2. Drain.
3. Transfer to a bowl.
4. Stir in the rest of the ingredients.
5. Process at 115 degrees F for 90 minutes.
6. Flip and break into smaller pieces.
7. Dry at 105 degrees F for 8 hours.

Tomato & Flaxseed Crackers

Preparation Time: 20 minutes
Dehydration Time: 8 hours
Servings: 24

Ingredients:

- 1 cup flaxseed
- 8sun-dried tomatoes
- 1 bell pepper, chopped
- 1tablespoon olive oil
- Salt to taste
- 2 tomatoes, chopped
- 1 onion, chopped
- 1 clove garlic, crushed through garlic press
- ¼ cup dried oregano leaves, crushed
- Salt and pepper to taste

Method:

1. Place the flaxseed in a bowl.
2. In another bowl, combine the remaining ingredients.
3. Stir in the flaxseeds.
4. Combine all the ingredients in the food processor.
5. Pulse until fully combined.
6. Spread the mixture in the Food Dehydrator.
7. Process at 110 degrees F for 12 hours.

CONCLUSION

Incorporating the age-old practices of food dehydration takes full advantage of what nature offers. Whether you're preserving seasonal crops or making protein-packed camping snacks, this dehydrator cookbook takes you through the ins and outs of dehydrating, storing, and rehydrating a wide variety of foods.

The Dehydrator Cookbook for Beginners contains everything you need to know to get the greatest value from a home dehydrator. The easy-to-follow drying instructions along with time guidelines make even a novice cook feel like a seasoned professional.